BREAKING APPLE

PATRICIA McCAW

Published by Cinnamon Press
Meirion House
Tanygrisiau
Blaenau Ffestiniog
Gwynedd, LL41 3SU
www.cinnamonpress.com

The right of Patricia McCaw to be identified as author of this work has been asserted by her in accordance with the Copyright, Designs and Patent Act, 1988. Copyright © 2018 Patricia McCaw. ISBN: 978-1-78864-037-4
British Library Cataloguing in Publication Data. A CIP record for this book can be obtained from the British Library.
All rights reserved. No part of this publication may be reproduced, stored in a retrieval system, or transmitted in any form or by any means, electronic, mechanical, photocopying, recording or otherwise without the prior written permission of the publishers. This book may not be lent, hired out, resold or otherwise disposed of by way of trade in any form of binding or cover other than that in which it is published, without the prior consent of the publishers.
Designed and typeset in Palatino by Cinnamon Press.
Cover design by Jan Fortune. Printed in Poland
Cinnamon Press is represented in the UK by Inpress Ltd and in Wales by the Welsh Books Council

Acknowledgements

'Stage Fright' won the Grierson Verse Prize, 2006, and was published in *Northwords Now* 2007, also published in the anthology of *Best of Creative Writing*, Edinburgh University Masters, 2006; an earlier version of 'Holiday Girls' was published in *Etchings*, Ilura Press, 2007; 'Feeding a Rescued Gannet' was Highly Commended in Yeovil International Literary Competition and also published in the Yeovil Literary Prize 2013 anthology of prize-winners for 2012&2013; 'Holding a Cord' was published in *Gutter* magazine, 2012; 'Starfall' was published in *Irish Literary Review*, 2014; 'Cutting the Strings' was published in *Poetry News*, Poetry Society as one of the winners in its competition, 2017; 'Light of the Shore' was shortlisted in Ver Poets' summer competition, 2017; 'Lines Not Learnt' was published in *Orbis*, autumn, 2017.

Thanks to Jan Fortune and all at Cinnamon Press, and special gratitude to David Mark Williams, a fine poet and teacher, for his guidance and encouragement throughout; also to Edinburgh's Other Writers and to Edinburgh's Pomegranate, and to Liam, who as a child, thought my rhyming stories were poetry and asked for more.

Contents

Ride Of Her Life	7
From Under Her Feet	8
Holiday Girls	10
Searching for the Signal	11
Feeding A Rescued Gannet	12
Becoming Dodo	13
Star Fall	14
Breaking Apple	15
Stage Fright	16
Preservation	17
A Hard Pruning	18
Lines Not Learnt	20
Holding A Cord	22
Playing For Time	23
Relative Disappearances	24
Cutting The Strings	26
All That They Gave Me	27
Snails	28
Light Of The Shore	30
Between the Rims	31
In Cold Blood	32
Eyes Tuned to a Dying Frequency	33
A Slow Depression Blankets Friends	34
Message from the Margins	35

*In memory of my parents, Bridie and Robert,
who first introduced me to the mysteries of love and learning,
and dedicating this book, with all my love, to Lorna,
who teaches me that imagination is the greatest dancer.*

Breaking Apple

Ride of Her Life

She taps the closed door of the north Down bus
as he counts the day's takings from the big leather bag.
He double-checks his machine—he likes things correct.

Have you found a pair of glasses?
So the history goes.

He tips back his peaked hat, sees a sleek Rita Hayworth
(whose curves will consolidate to a friendly fourteen stone).
He's slight as a jockey (who will box as a feather-weight).

He laughs, *I have.*
And so, the race is on.

They probe each other's history—
both miss the soil and sea but not the stones of a southern farm.
They've travelled north for its post-war promise—both here for the ride.

My mother straightens her stockings and unbuttons
an austerity coat that reveals just a clavicle.
The wooing excites the pounds deep in dad's bag.

Oh, she's smitten right then by eyes blue as the Arctic—
no reflection of dark bog-man, or a future imperfect—
just a wheel that is cart-sized, and steered by his hand.

She nods *Let's begin* to the man who
would never lay a finger on her—
so she said.

From Under Her Feet

The hands, the foot,
           across the room where
baby sister crawls,

legs sausage-plump
like Bess, my doll's,

scuffing up tufts of rug
that daddy, mammy made

when first engaged,
           his hand, her hand
big over small, loop over hook.

I'm just turned four and run
           to catch the feet that rode
me round the room.

His shoes, like winds,
           slap past the rug
and leave me by the slamming door.

The wool's messed up, and fat
           with bacon, bread, where
a flying saucer landed.

Mammy's hands
and daddy's feet.

Our baby screams and stands to walk
           and mammy's leg swings high
and baby's bottom spins.

She sails through space, crying,
        flying, and in my mind
a click, a camera shutter,

snaps fast the foot that hurtles
        space and time
to join the hands that hurt one better,

snaps fast in me the shoe,
the foot, the rug.

Holiday Girls

It's summer and my schoolbag's lost itself forever
as we work five days, not just Saturdays anymore.

Mr McGuffin, his eyes bright as morning above
the moustache, lets me weigh sweets,
cut Warhorse tobacco for men with hands like coal.

Miss McGuffin, his flat-chested sister, eyes canny,
strokes a lip light with feathers, talks Scottish, soft and strange.

The Belfast Telegraph van screeches outside, throws a load
of 'pinks' for men desperate for the racing news.

A woman lashes me, tongue-sharp for I've given her thruppence short.

My sister, younger and prettier, gets off an hour earlier
on account of being twelve.

I hear Mr Cardy, a customer, whisper to her,
If you like, I'll take you home.

I watch his old grey face and think of his wife sick at home.

I see his car outside the window, blotting the lighthouse view,
its bonnet face blank and dull.
I tell him, *She's to stay with me.* His eyes look fishy.

My sister waits on the seawall kicking her heels, fierce temper on her face.
Later, I see Mr Cardy's motorcar moved up to Giovanelli's Café.

He comes out, and carries an ice-cream cone, one in each hand.
He sits in the car, eating them both, slowly, before he goes home.

Searching for the Signal

You won't get much reception here,
the land surveyor says
as she records lost lands and missing vegetation.

In this national park, all hills and dips
and anxious sheep, I scale higher ground
seeking conductors of transmission

but all calls fail.

We make a career, you and I
of missing each other
in the wrong place, the wrong time

tongues tied, tampering with subtext,
antennae broken.

We tap out morse in place of speech
on remote keypads,
playing with numbers, not feelings

using words of one syllable, one letter:
R U there?
Descending to spaces.

Now, I've reached the highest peak
whirling the phone skywards
but silence chokes the airways.

All that's left is a long slide down
over ancient moss and bones

hardening to stone.

Feeding a Rescued Gannet

My manager hands me a fish with 'Mind the beak!'
but the eyes trap me, adrift as the Arctic.
He's blown off course, no pain, no break,

they claim, but I see something tragic.
Blue blazes me, rim within rim.
He lunges, jabs, denies he's sick,

still claiming his right where he can't be king.
After I crossed the Irish Sea
I lay on the Galloway Rhins

watching gannets patrol, alert and free,
fierce border guards with tilting wings
to dive for fish, repel the returnee

who migrate, re-seek, and spin in rings,
doomed never to find the landing strip.
I nod at the bird—he bows and sings,

gapes, surrenders. Brine soaks my lip.

Becoming Dodo

I'm branching into bird
my voice a chirp
bold nose shading
to beak

hands like claws
that snag on blankets
sheer as clouds.
Feathers sprout on chin

once held high and bare
eye-brows crest and swoop.
I'm moving towards extinction
wings a vestige

of soaring flights
and cradling young,
eggs an abstract,
my nest a palimpsest.

As a child I loved the dodo,
a giant with a bright-gold face
but time showed only
a pigeon without wings.

I have plans for my flight,
controls at the ready.
I won't display behind glass
for visitors to pity

or linger too long
with no one to kill me.
I've set timer and sat nav
for the long migration home.

Star Fall

We stayed up half the night
beneath the velux, waiting
for the shower of the decade,
or century, I forget.

Lying on the old mattress, dragged
from the bed that had
no view,
our heads twin-frozen.

We were seeking torrents, shreds
of long-dead rocks and dust,
physical reminders of where
we'd begun,

foresights of rockets,
home perhaps.

What stays in my mind
is the old bald moon

glaring right at us
through the occult glass.
It kept the stars on a leash all night,
determined not to let one thing fall.

Breaking Apple

Out in the wild of a walk, we don't obey
the regular mealtimes,
we are not measured against each other
by the size of our plates. Instead
my dog and I break apple.

As I chop with the knife or just bite
she cranes forward to trap the sweetness
eyes wide as a cat,
hushed like no-breath
while I eat around the core.

The gloss-capped seeds won't have her,
those star-shaped channels that beg teeth to bite.
I tease out segments, prise out and dispose
of the cyanide pills,
savour her grateful crunch.

We're like the first creatures when breaking apple.

Stage Fright

The worst part was burying our dog,
my arms long, bearing her into the air.
I'd wrapped her, a god's gift, in red cloth,
choreographing her exit, like a director.
My lover scattered her with quicklime
and a square stone, in case of foxes.
We crouched like Sodomites, salted in time.
Seventeen years, Belle always beside us.

In the wee hours a reminding bell tolled our crime:
She was too warm—maybe she was conscious?
My lover turned over, and I, at first light
crept out. The earth was crawling worms, a mime,
a cast of death; she a prop, no more, no less.
I, now an extra, suffering stage fright.

Preservation

His head was a soaked sponge, grey-splashed
from buckets of northern rain spilling over thick plastic
that he liked to call a coat.
More effigy than man, framed in the doorway,
her mother would have hissed *Bogman* under her breath.

Her mother had never seen the real bog man
like she had in Aarhus. Like a buried sun
he was bronze corrugations, not seeming human
but a whole new breed. A pity the damp had spoilt him
apart from fingerprints that remained his own.

The lead dripped in his fist, the dog's eyes desperate.
She had to ask, *Has she done her business?*
His head drooped no.
They'd have to brave the storm again.
She felt like one of the Furies.

The door closed on a curtain of sleet,
the turn of a heel leaving its imprint.

A Hard Pruning

You exchange work shoes, worn thin,
for boots in the Botanics,
freed from the thicket
of loud lights, fading courage.

Now you choose dark aisles
where goldfinch, firecrest and robins' young
flit beneath branches so massed
even loppers won't do.

You squeeze and slice each shrub grown large,
crowded mistakes deep in this Chinese hillside,
too wild for visitors who *Can't see a thing!*

The gardener shows where elm seeded, pushing forward
their newest heirs, and tells you
Cut hard, let light find what's over-shadowed, rare.
You prune to preserve, not to show pretty.

You reach for other weapons that sever the living
as well as the dead, crashing down rich-berried boughs
to their tree-like knees,
to rip, extract and all the other surgery.

Plants hide, light-shy, light-hungry,
parts at war with themselves
like you,
an unstable switch in a room grown dark.

I hold your hand, along curved paths,
brandishing tools in broad thrusts
and ruthless sundering.
We conjure giant cracks
to split the sky.

We pull and we burn,
muscles stretched,
twisted beyond endurance.
Each day, we show up,
bandaged hearts leaking.

What matters is the clearing.

Lines Not Learnt

Sky

Nobody's looking at the sky yet
although we're waiting for the plane.

I'm standing by the back door
not putting the washing out
while his widow, last week's wife
leans against their shed
which is stuffed with things he wouldn't throw out.

We've not prepared a speech yet.
We're forming a line for the plane.

The widow's mouth is blowing smoke
past neighbours, kin, and tells about
the empty seat. The airline charged
for the surplus case while his body stayed abroad.

Nobody's mentioned dark clouds yet,
our breath holding for the coffin-plane.

Line

His holiday wash is still flapping on the line,
baggy shorts, tee-shirts red, white and gold.

I hear her thoughts—how the sun still shines
and the blackbird whistles.
Why did Spring delay
until now, two weeks too late

and how their bench for two
will squeeze her out
with family sat too tight to hide
the space that's just been born.

Last night, the daughter's car crept down our street,
a rehearsal of the final act,
lights turned off,
her lines not learnt.

Holding a Cord

It was very good of them, really.
A time of terrible grief for us all
but he was their son, and I
was someone he'd always love,
he told me
lying on one elbow before the fire
in his place—he always burned coal
where I was electric.
Thirty years the same place. Me too.
We had coincidences like that all along the way.
Two big men we were, each a moustache
at varied times. Taken for twins more than once
though I had six years on him.
That made it worse.

I half-expected to be discouraged,
let down gently, told *It's a family affair, Sam.*
[some guff—the da wants it small, close relatives]
But they took the ground from my feet when
he pulled me to him like a long-lost son,
never said a word that made sense but
held out a cord to me, and the six of us
lowered away, one black back.
I wanted to jump in after him.

It took the death of him to light the life in me.
I didn't go to the funeral tea, out of respect.

Playing for Time

She lifts the lid of the neighbour's piano
presses fingers on hammers
that strike strings in her soul.

She had meant to learn each decade,
now's far too late,
but she's time on her hands.

The teacher is stern as a metronome,
tilts her shoulders to *sway like a biker,*
insists she could *play like Tchaikovsky.*

She doubts she could live that long.

The teacher grabs her wrists—no time for arthritis—
hands must work together
but they keep two minds, as they always did.

Opposites damn the melody in her soul.

Notes are runes that give up meaning
through sharps, flats, naturals.
Teacher urges, *Press as if penetrating flesh.*

Always sing along. Cantabile.

Forearms drop in freefall,
suave flow is composed from harsh steps—
put more effort in so less effort shows.

Contrary, contrary.

The clock ticks and she never looks,
she strokes the keys with crippled bone
and follows her place on the line.

Relative Disappearances

And so it all falls away:

the chickens stuffed
buttermilk bread
piled-bowls of dried-out oranges.

All falls after the wife goes.

Next the house and car's gone
for a pensioner's flat and a fridge
full of tins

until

the food's a chore
of barely tasted meals

fruit grown soft from visitors
that don't come back
thank God.

Mould multiplies.

Eggs keep their interest
but only just.
The fridge click's a dinner bell
for a spoonful of beans.

Crumbs reassemble
into rocks of loaves.
The stomach's heart fails.

The body feels its weakness

but the daughter can't know.

Skin's thin on the hands
and blue round the nose.

Still, the mirror eye winks:
It's all right

there's not much wrong
when breath still travels through it.

Cutting the Strings

I'm mute now in the public ward,
waiting, wanting at bitter last for you to die
easy-out and instant
like a best-loved dog.

Your flesh is rusting iron,
the tang of borrowed blood,
sacs of it splashing your veins,
out again past the crippled backdoor.

Nothing can save you now.

Needle in, needle out, they sewed your suit,
frilling flesh round a heart made huge by a hundred strangers.

I see your chest-bones, Dad,
sharp-arched, bare bones gone to earth.

I want to lift you hard by your heels, slapping the life out of you.

All That They Gave Me

Two soiled pyjamas,
a bloodstained vest,
one flattened shaving brush,
a tin of Steradent.

I'd kissed dad's hand
as life's swelling died
releasing rings that he'd prised
to no effect only moments earlier.

A child played Game Boy in the next bed,
a man sobbed across the way
but not me.
I'm stone.

A coffin of words lies between us.

Once, he gave me coins he'd framed
in glass and wood—
polished silver crowns and farthings
They'll be worth something some day.

Now, nothing is left but his last effects
and cards and roses he'd wished to pulp.
No use, I hear him mutter
no damn use at all.

Snails

The least arthritic hand unwinds
the tangled sheet,
    levering you up
past a duvet that's winter-weight
    all year round
and hell in summer.

You are muscle, gelatinous,
right out of your shell,
    blind in the dark
and slow from the pain,
    unstable bones that took
on an object and lost.

The night's load is hard
in the shedding,
    all ghosts of your mother
when she stood tall and straight,
    cooking winkles from the beach
where she built castles large and strong.

She had a knack with the pin,
you still taste that saline chew.
    The best were cockles, girlhood frills,
shells bonny as bonnets
    then dinner and oysters,
no bones that could hurt.

Your backyard oozes gastropods
reliable as rain,
    horned creepers dragging bustles,
seeking sweetness in greenness,
    the last of the rhubarb
overlooked by a burlapped gardener.

You grip shell and watch
how the flesh shrinks back,
    fling it high, imagine smorgasbord,
a feast on the shed's roof
    where songs are heard from blackbirds
who grieve on so little soil.

Light of the Shore

In the Celtic calendar, the longest day of the year

Bone white sand, graveyard of shells.

Lagoon beach
diamonds on the sea.

Red dulse, leather slaps,
when dried a popcorn feast.

Candy-headed pinks soften
harsh marram grass, green anchors underground.

My mother's wheelchair churns ancient pram-tracks,
covered-over castles of falling-down sands that she
would build with water until they stood, and my tears dried.

Her fingers lift, reed-thin, and wave towards mine.

This longest day is too short.

Between the Rims, Portpatrick

The pale yachts have berthed from Ireland,
umbilical fuel sharper than ozone,
named for Tara, Oisin, Finn Macoul.

The seawall nests guillemots, scarlet-footed
paddlers, expanding circles, back
to harbour as tide tumbles hard.

From high etched steps, day-trippers, bolder
than me, shed shoes and troubles to climb
and hang off basalt twists, between air and water.

I climb on and the steps ground me,
the first carved GENESIS. This is what
we're made of : Mineral Water Dust

At the last step, hidden between gorse
and bramble, the name trips me:
DONAGHADEE   22 MILES

The spelling is wrong but its long tongue
is my own, the place where I was born,
longing for here, its twin across the sea.

There's a man still there, on the opposite
shore, this side of death, musing on ghosts maybe
of childish hands and feet on the endless seawall.

And I want to push this land over there
and drag that place over here to join
them both in one life, sealing the rims.

On my path down, boats steer out again,
flags tearing,
white-headed against the wind.

In Cold Blood

Swans don't always mate for life:
the one our way took a new pen
and kicked the old one out
after ten long years –

no eggs, it seems,
last Easter-time.

The new bit's throned on the nest
sorting straw from dross and paddling down
a firm foundation while he picks daffodils
teasing out the finest foliage,
mincing green stalks smug as a butcher.

I watched them from the canal bank, curving necks,
beak to bill, in a perfect heart.

They found the old one's corpse
some time later,
no fox or poison in the frame.

Nothing to be blamed or mourned.

Eyes Tuned to a Dying Frequency

I found a dead lamb, last week, strung from a tree
and trudged through mud to confirm the corpse.
It was nothing worse than a shrugged-off fleece—
no nerves, no bone, bleached as a childhood ghost.

Today, near a loch, I spotted a swan's remains,
killed by a fox, or a human at worst.
With each step towards the sight, my eyes
retuned and slaughter faded into melting snow.

Each countryside trip I'm tricked into tragedy
or something foreshadowing it, unlike at home
watching wildlife where I never see death
but keep the remote close, under control.

I've seen how hearts can die in a tangle
of tubes, fur, a mess of feathers,
leaving my own to soldier on,
shouldering all that's gone wrong.

A Slow Depression Blankets Friends

Your house is cold.
Plants crinkle from no love.
The cat cries.
You beat a slow drum.
The mood is vacuum.

The postman calls, *Anybody there?*
a ghost at the flap, teeth like vice.
A box is delivered, pharmaceuticals.

You sit for hours.
The syrup settles into ice-time
faint impressions on your chin.
It could be early, could be bed-time.

You say you want nothing to mean nothing
and if it could be guaranteed
you'd do it now
pull the trigger.

If friend means friend, you say
I'd trip your current, pull the lever,
count down from ten
explode you back again.

Message from the Margins

I was looking for some thing
some sign from my mother
some signal from Charon's boat
on which she'd left
without bags or warning.

Hard to forgive her.

I searched the beach where she'd brought me
from the birth-house, it was
still the same sea, its sands oyster-grey.
There were no shells to be found
or bottles from far shores.

I left the sea behind and walked
towards the woods of deep country
where I'd lived as a child.
The roads were bare, no traffic,
the old home swallowed by furze.

I turned back on to the blank road, and a shell
lay on the tarmac, before my feet, miles
from its source—a huge whelk spilt over my palm.
Dark pigments showed great age, dirt showing
travel over oceans, time. It was whole, pink.

I held it to my ear.